# Advanced Beginner's English Reader

*Exploring culture and building communication skills*

Barbara Dogger

**National Textbook Company**
*a division of* NTC/CONTEMPORARY PUBLISHING COMPANY
Lincolnwood, Illinois USA

*Many thanks to Rae Lamberton, my typist and friend.
She made the writing of this reader and manual so much easier.*

**Illustrations by Phil Kantz**

ISBN: 0-8442-5377-4

Published by National Textbook Company,
a division of NTC/Contemporary Publishing Company,
4255 West Touhy Avenue,
Lincolnwood (Chicago), Illinois 60646-1975 U.S.A.
© 1992 by NTC/Contemporary Publishing Company
All rights reserved. No part of this book may be reproduced,
stored in a retrieval system, or transmitted in any form or by any means,
electronic, mechanical, photocopying, recording, or otherwise,
without prior permission of the publisher.
Manufactured in the United States of America.

8 9 0 VP 10 9 8 7 6 5

# Preface

*Advanced Beginner's English Reader* is designed to make learning enjoyable for high beginning and low intermediate students in junior and senior high school. Through twenty-seven lively readings students explore various aspects of American culture. They are introduced to American teenagers and their families and friends, and follow their daily adventures at school—both in the classroom and in extracurricular activities—and at home, at work, and at play. Students will follow the events with interest and will relate to typical experiences such as enrolling at a new school, trying out for a team, going to a school dance, getting a driver's license, preparing for college, and applying for a part-time job.

The readings are filled with natural, authentic language and dialogues and are followed by reading comprehension and vocabulary exercises, which review and reinforce the concepts and vocabulary introduced in each chapter.

This high-interest reader can be used with students who have finished the first book in this series, *Beginner's English Reader,* and are ready for more challenging sentence structures and vocabulary, and with all advanced beginning students who want to develop their reading and communication skills and gain insights into American culture.

# Contents

1. The First Day of School — 1
2. The School Schedule — 3
3. Unpacking — 5
4. Shopping — 8
5. Dave Goes out for Basketball — 11
6. Melissa Tries out for the Band — 13
7. Dave Gets a Driver's License — 15
8. Growing up Fast — 17
9. A Job Interview — 19
10. A Part-Time Job — 22
11. Getting to Know Tom and Jill — 25
12. A Day at the Beach — 28
13. Friendly Competition — 30
14. Three's a Crowd — 33
15. Dating: Part 1 — 35
16. Dating: Part 2 — 38
17. Expect the Unexpected — 41
18. The School Dance — 44
19. Some Exciting News — 47
20. The Welcoming Party — 49
21. Carmen and Jill Become Friends — 52
22. Carmen Meets Mrs. Schroeder — 55
23. Family Matters — 58
24. The College Entrance Exam — 61
25. Planning for College — 63
26. The Family Trip — 66
27. A Special Dinner — 69

# 1 The First Day of School

David and Melissa Jackson recently moved with their parents from their hometown in Ohio to Briartown, Pennsylvania. They are learning their way around their new city. Today they are walking to their new school.

As they approach the school, Dave and Melissa see several students outside. Some of the students say hello as Dave and Melissa walk past. They enter the school and find the principal's office. The principal, Mr. Rodriguez, shakes their hands.

"Welcome to Lincoln High School," he says. "I'll get your schedules and help you find your first-period classes."

Dave and Melissa follow Mr. Rodriguez to two classrooms at the end of a long hall.

"Melissa, this is your English class for the first period. David, this is your algebra class. Oh, yes! Here are your class schedules. When you finish this period, just look at your schedules to find your next classes."

"Thanks, Mr. Rodriguez," says Dave.

"Yes, we really appreciate your help," adds Melissa.

"I'm happy to help. I hope you both enjoy your first day at Lincoln High School."

**A. Answer the questions.**
1. Where did Dave and Melissa move with their family?
2. Where are they walking today?
3. Whom do they see as they approach the school? What do the students say?
4. Whose office do they visit in the school?
5. Is Mr. Rodriguez friendly? How does he greet Melissa and Dave?
6. Where does Mr. Rodriguez take them?
7. What class does Melissa have during the first period?
8. What class does Dave have during the first period?
9. How will Dave and Melissa find their next classes?
10. What do Dave and Melissa say to Mr. Rodriguez?

**B. Complete the sentences with these vocabulary words. If necessary, change the form of a word to make it agree with the other parts of the sentence. The first one is done for you.**

a. algebra
b. (to) appreciate
c. (to) approach
d. class schedule
e. first period
f. hometown
g. (to) learn one's way around
h. office
i. principal
j. several
k. (to) shake hands

1. The friends <u>shook hands</u> when they saw each other on the street.
2. Joseph returned to his _____, where he grew up.
3. _____ is Susan's favorite subject.
4. The _____ dismissed all the students for the day. Then she walked back into her _____.
5. Adam followed his _____ carefully during the first week of school. He also _____ the new school.
6. James was almost late for the _____ because he woke up late.
7. When Mai _____ the group of friends, _____ of them said hi.
8. Diane _____ the help she got from her new friends. She thanked them.

# 2 The School Schedule

After first period, Dave and Melissa meet in the hall.

"Boy! That algebra teacher, Mrs. Shum, is really tough. She gave us a lot of homework, too. We have a whole chapter to read and ten exercises to complete before tomorrow. She explains everything well, but I'll have to study most of the evening for her assignment. And that's only one class!"

"You're going to have a busy year, Dave," says Melissa. "My English teacher, Mr. Baxton, is really nice. We're reading the play *Julius Caesar* now. It's a difficult play, but Mr. Baxton makes it clear. I think I'm going to like this class a lot."

"You're lucky, Melissa!" exclaims Dave. "Oh, well. Where's your next class?"

"It's in room 214, but I don't know where that is yet," answers Melissa. "It's Spanish, and I'm excited about studying another language. What do you have next, Dave?"

"I have PE next. That will be a nice break after algebra! I hear that the PE instructor is tough too, but that's okay. You know how much I love sports."

"Oh no, there's the bell. It's time to be in class!"

"You're right. See you later, Melissa. Good luck!"

"Thanks, Dave. You, too."

**A. Answer the following questions.**
1. Where do Dave and Melissa meet after their first-period classes?
2. What does Dave say about his algebra teacher, Mrs. Shum?
3. Does Dave have any homework for tomorrow?
4. What does Melissa say about Mr. Baxton, her English teacher?
5. What play are the students reading in Mr. Baxton's class? Is it difficult?
6. What is Melissa's next class? Is she going to like this subject?
7. What is Dave's next class? Why is he going to like it?

**B. Complete the sentences with these vocabulary words. If necessary, change the form of a word to make it agree with the other parts of the sentence.**

a. assignment
b. chapter
c. homework
d. PE
e. play
f. Spanish
g. (to) study
h. tough

1. Arun's favorite subject is _____ because he likes sports.
2. Marie likes her _____ class because she enjoys learning a second language. For tomorrow she must study the next _____ of her book.
3. Larry and Sylvia usually do their _____ right after school. They can relax after they complete their _____.
4. Sean always _____ a lot for his algebra tests.
5. Linda liked her math teacher, but she thought he was _____.
6. The _____ *Romeo and Juliet* is a famous love story.

# 3 Unpacking

"Hi, Mom! Hi, Dad! How's it going?" Dave and Melissa arrive home from school and greet their parents.

"We're fine, but we're tired," answers Mr. Jackson. "We spent the whole day unpacking. The kitchen and living room are just about finished. How was your day at school?"

"Not bad," answers Dave.

"It's a nice school," says Melissa. "We'll tell you all about it at dinner."

"Good! Did you see those boxes in the entryway with your names on them? They go in your rooms, kids."

"Ugh!" moans Melissa. "Just what I was planning to do after my first day at a new school!"

"Well, I'll help you carry the boxes to your rooms. Then you can unpack them after you do your homework. Or you can even wait until the weekend to unpack."

"That sounds like a great idea, Dad! Thanks!" Melissa gives her father a big kiss and heads toward the kitchen for an after-school snack. Dave follows her.

**A. Answer the following questions.**
1. What do Dave and Melissa do when they get home from school?
2. What were Mr. and Mrs. Jackson doing all day?
3. Which rooms are almost finished?
4. What does Mr. Jackson want Melissa and Dave to do with their boxes?
5. Are Dave and Melissa happy about this? What does Melissa say?
6. Does Mr. Jackson offer to help? What will he do?
7. Finally, what does Mr. Jackson suggest to Dave and Melissa?
8. Where do Melissa and Dave go next? Why?

**B. Complete the sentences with these vocabulary words. If necessary, change the form of a word to make it agree with the other parts of the sentence.**

a. (to) arrive
b. entryway
c. (to) greet
d. (to) head
e. idea
f. just about
g. (to) moan
h. snack
i. (to) spend
j. (to) unpack
k. (to) wait

1. Marci and Matt were very hungry when they got home, so they ate an after-school _____.
2. James _____ because his broken ankle hurt.
3. Gloria _____ the whole day inside because it was raining.
4. Bill _____ home from work and stood in the _____ looking for his family. Then he _____ toward the kitchen.
5. Francine _____ her grandmother with a hug. "Dinner is _____ ready," she said. "Why don't you _____ after we eat?"
6. Ariel _____ for the bus for almost forty minutes.
7. Do you have any _____ when Jack will be home?

# 4 Shopping

It's Saturday morning. Melissa and her mother, Helen Jackson, are going grocery shopping. They arrive at the store with their shopping list.

"Melissa, will you please get a shopping cart for us?" asks Mrs. Jackson. "There are a lot of items on this list, and we will certainly need a cart to carry them all."

"Okay, I'll get one."

Melissa selects a cart and wheels it toward her mother. Then they head to the produce section. They pick out broccoli, bananas, oranges, and Mr. Jackson's favorite fruit—grapes. They finish selecting fresh fruits and vegetables and go to the meat and fish counter and the dairy case. Mrs. Jackson selects a beef roast, some pork chops, and some fish fillets. From the dairy case, Melissa gets three pounds of cheese and a carton of milk.

Next, they go to the bread and cereal aisle. Melissa picks up a box of Oat Bits, the family's favorite cereal. Mrs. Jackson selects two loaves of bread.

Finally, they finish selecting items and go to the checkout counter. Mrs. Jackson pays for the groceries. The big job of family grocery shopping is finished for the week. Now they can have some fun.

**A. Answer the following questions.**
1. What are Melissa and her mother doing this morning?
2. What do they bring with them to the store?
3. What does Melissa get first? Why?
4. What do they pick out in the produce section? What is Mr. Jackson's favorite fruit?
5. What is produce?
6. What does Mrs. Jackson select from the meat and fish counter?
7. What does Melissa get from the dairy case?
8. What do Melissa and her mother pick up in the bread and cereal aisle?
9. What does Mrs. Jackson do at the checkout counter?
10. After they finish their grocery shopping, what can Melissa and her mother do?

**B. Complete the sentences with these vocabulary words. If necessary, change the form of a word to make it agree with the other parts of the sentence.**

a. aisle
b. cart
c. checkout counter
d. dairy
e. favorite
f. (to) pick out
g. produce
h. (to) select
i. shopping list

1. A _____ helps you remember what to buy at the grocery store.
2. A shopping _____ is a large basket on wheels.
3. In a grocery store, the food is displayed on shelves. Customers walk down each _____ as they _____ what they want to buy.
4. You can find fresh fruits and vegetables in the _____ section. Milk and cheese are in the _____ aisle.
5. What is your _____ kind of cereal?
6. After you _____ your groceries, you can pay for them at the _____.

# 5 Dave Goes out for Basketball

Dave and Melissa see each other between classes at school.
"I'm so nervous that I can't sit down," says Dave.
"What's wrong?" asks Melissa.
"Well, basketball tryouts are this afternoon, and I really want to get on the team."
"Weren't you practicing all last week?" asks Melissa.
"I practiced every afternoon for the last month!" exclaims Dave. "Jeff has a basketball hoop at his house, so he and I practice there every day."

Well, I know you're a good athlete, Dave! With all that practice, you should do just fine."

"I hope so. We'll see," says Dave.

"Well, time to get to class. See you later," says Melissa.

"Bye," says Dave.

"Good luck," adds Melissa.

"Thanks. I need it."

At home later that afternoon, Melissa asks, "Well, what happened, Dave?"

"Oh, nothing."

"I don't believe you, Dave! Did you make the team?"

"Yup," says Dave with a big grin on his face.

Melissa shrieks and gives her brother a big hug. "I knew you could do it! I'm so proud of you!"

"Oh, it was nothing," says Dave.

"Sure!" laughs Melissa.

### A. Answer the following questions.
1. Why is Dave nervous?
2. How often does he practice?
3. Where does he practice? Why?
4. What does Melissa tell Dave?
5. Does Dave make the team?
6. How does Dave feel?
7. How does Melissa feel?

### B. Complete the sentences with these vocabulary words. If necessary, change the form of a word to make it agree with the other parts of the sentence.

a. athlete      e. (to) practice
b. hoop         f. proud
c. (to) hug     g. (to) shriek
d. nervous      h. tryout

During the (1.) _____ for the basketball team, Lana jumped and threw the ball through the (2.) _____ several times. She wasn't (3.) _____, because she (4.) _____ a lot. After the tryouts, she felt (5.) _____ because she did her best. Her friend Paula (6.) _____ and ran up to (7.) _____ her. Paula exclaimed, "What a good (8.) _____ you are!"

# 6 Melissa Tries out for the Band

Melissa and Dave are sitting at the breakfast table before school.

"Dave, you did so well yesterday! I'm very proud of you for making the basketball team."

"Well, I do feel good about it. But I was pretty nervous at this time yesterday."

"That's the way I feel this morning," Melissa replies. "Today it's my turn to try out for the concert band."

"Wow, Melissa! This is a big week for both of us! But don't worry. You're a wonderful trumpet player. I'm sure you can beat the competition."

"We'll see. The other trumpet players in this school are very good. I know it will be more difficult than it was at our old school."

"I still think you'll do great, Melissa! Hey, it's time to get going! It's almost time for class."

"You're right, Dave. Well, wish me luck."
"I do, Melissa. I know you can do it!"
(*later that day*)
"Well, what happened, Melissa?"
"What happened? I'm exhausted, Dave! I told you the other trumpet players were good, didn't I? The competition was very stiff. But I was lucky. I did make it into the concert band."
"That's great, Melissa! I knew you could do it. Just wait! You're going to show the rest of the band what good playing really is!"
"Thanks."

**A. Answer the following questions.**
1. Where are Dave and Melissa sitting?
2. Who is nervous this morning? Why?
3. What does Dave tell Melissa?
4. What does Melissa say about the other trumpet players in their new school?
5. After the tryouts, what does Melissa tell Dave?
6. Then what does Dave tell Melissa?

**B. Complete the sentences with these vocabulary words. If necessary, change the form of a word to make it agree with the other parts of the sentence.**

a. (to) beat
b. competition
c. concert band
d. exhausted
e. (to) make it
f. stiff
g. trumpet player

Lisa and Mike were talking about the tryouts for the (1.) _____. Lisa, a (2.) _____, was worried about the (3.) _____ (4.) _____. "Don't worry," said Mike. "You play very well. I'm sure you'll (5.) _____ the other players."

Lisa practiced every evening that week. On Friday she was ready for the tryouts. The next day she saw Mike.

"How are you, Lisa?" he asked.
"I'm (6.) _____," she said with a smile, "but I (7.) _____ into the concert band!"

# 7 Dave Gets a Driver's License

Dave practiced his driving with his mom and dad for a month. Now he feels ready to take the test for his driver's license. He and his dad enter the office of the Department of Transportation.

"May I help you?" asks Lt. Nelson, the police officer at the desk.

"Yes," Mr. Jackson replies. "My son wants to take his driving test. What do we do first?"

"There are two parts to the driver's test," replies Lt. Nelson. "First, he'll take the written test. Then we'll go for a drive to see how he does behind the wheel."

"That's fine. When can he begin?"

"Right now," replies the officer. "Young man, please come this way. We'll get you started on the written test over here."

Dave follows Lt. Nelson into a room filled with desks. Thirty minutes later he returns with a smile on his face.

"I passed, Dad!"

"That's great, son!"

Lt. Nelson walks up to them. "Dave passed the written test with flying colors," he announces. Turning to Dave, he asks, "Now are you ready to do some driving?"

"Sure! I'm ready!"

"Good! Please follow me out to the parking lot. We'll get you started right away."

"See you later, Dad!"

"Good luck, Dave."

"Thanks."

A. **Answer the following questions.**
1. What did Dave do for a month?
2. What does he feel ready to do now?
3. Where does he go? Who goes with him?
4. What are the two parts to the driving test?
5. Which part does Dave take first? How long does the test take?
6. Why does Dave have a smile on his face after the test?
7. What does Lt. Nelson say when he returns?
8. Where does Dave go next? Why?

B. **Complete the sentences with these vocabulary words. If necessary, change the form of a word to make it agree with the other parts of the sentence.**
   a. (to) drive
   b. driver's license
   c. parking lot
   d. ready
   e. test
   f. wheel
   g. with flying colors

Jana practiced (1.) _____ for three months before she felt (2.) _____ to take her driving (3.) _____. When she took the written test, she passed (4.) _____. Then a police officer led her to the (5.) _____, where she took the test behind the (6.) _____. This part was more difficult, but Jana passed. Later that month, she received her (7.) _____ in the mail.

# 8 Growing up Fast

Dave bursts through the door. His dad is right behind him.
"I passed! Hey, Mom! Melissa! I passed my driving test!"
"Really, Dave?" cries Melissa. "That's terrific!"
"I'm very proud of you, Dave," says Mom.
"Thanks. You are now looking at the newest licensed driver in the Jackson family!"

"We are impressed!" says Melissa a little jealously. "Well, what are you going to do now that you have your license?"
"I'm going to get a part-time job after school," says Dave.
"You are?" asks his mother in surprise.
"Yup! I want to get a job so I have more spending money. I may even buy a car."

"Wow! That's thinking big," exclaims Melissa.

"Well, I don't know, David," says Dad. "We'll have to see about that. You're pretty busy in school right now. Let's take one step at a time."

"Well, can I at least borrow the family car once in a while?"

"Of course. We'll be able to work that out. For now, just relax and enjoy your success."

"Okay, Dad," replies Dave.

Dave and Melissa go into the living room. Mr. Jackson looks at his wife and says, "Our kids are growing up fast, aren't they, Helen?"

"Yes, they are," agrees Mrs. Jackson. "A little too fast sometimes."

**A. Answer the following questions.**
1. Why is Dave excited?
2. What does his mother say?
3. What does Melissa ask him?
4. What does Dave plan to do now that he has his driver's license?
5. What does Mr. Jackson think about Dave's plans?
6. What do Mr. and Mrs. Jackson say after Dave and Melissa go into the living room?

**B. Complete the sentences with these vocabulary words. If necessary, change the form of a word to make it agree with the other parts of the sentence.**

a. (to) borrow       d. jealous
b. (to) grow up      e. (to) relax
c. impressed         f. spending money

José was very (1.) _____ when Tina got her driver's license. He was also a little (2.) _____.

"(3.) _____, José," his mother said. "You're (4.) _____ fast. Soon you'll have your driver's license, too."

"When I learn to drive, will you let me (5.) _____ your car?" asked José.

"I'll think about it," his mother answered. "But if you start saving your (6.) _____ now, maybe you can buy your own car."

# 9 A Job Interview

Later that week, Dave enters Tackett's Shoe Shop. He sees a clerk at the front of the store and walks over to her.

"May I please speak with Mr. Tackett?" he asks. "I have a three o'clock appointment with him."

"Sure! May I have your name?"

"I'm Dave Jackson. I called yesterday about the job in your newspaper advertisement."

"Oh, sure! We're looking for someone to work evenings and Saturdays. Just a minute. I'll get Mr. Tackett."

A few minutes later, Mr. Tackett comes out of his office. He walks up and shakes Dave's hand.

"You're Dave Jackson, aren't you? Pleased to meet you. I understand that you're interested in our part-time sales job."

"Yes, I am," Dave answers. "I'm free after school and on Saturdays, and I am really interested in working for you."

"Well, let's see. What kind of work experience do you have?"

"Not any, really," says Dave. "But I'm willing to learn," he adds after a pause.

"I'm sure you are," says Mr. Tackett. "We need someone to work from five to nine on Thursday and Friday evenings and all day on Saturday—that is, from 10:00 A.M. to 6:00 P.M. How does that schedule sound?"

"It sounds great, Mr. Tackett! It will work out perfectly with school."

"Good! Now, we'll start you out at the minimum wage, of course."

"That's fine," responds Dave eagerly.

"We'll see how things go during the school year. If you continue to work for us during the summer, we can think about giving you a little raise."

"That would be terrific!"

"Well now, please fill out this application form. When you're finished, bring it back to my office and we'll discuss when you should begin."

"Okay. I'll be done with it in a few minutes."

"Good."

They shake hands. Mr. Tackett returns to his office. Dave sits down in a chair to fill out the application. "This will be a great place to work!" he thinks. "I'm so glad Mom and Dad finally agreed to let me get a job."

**A. Answer the following questions.**
1. When Dave walks into Tackett's Shoe Shop, whom does he see?
2. To whom does he want to speak? Why?
3. Where did Dave learn about the part-time job?
4. When is Dave free to work?
5. Does Dave have any work experience? What does he tell Mr. Tackett?
6. When does Mr. Tackett need someone to work? Is the schedule a good one for Dave?
7. How much money will Dave earn?
8. What is possible for Dave in the summer?
9. What does Mr. Tackett ask Dave to do?

B. Complete the sentences with these vocabulary words. If necessary, change the form of a word to make it agree with the other parts of the sentence.

a. advertisement
b. application form
c. appointment
d. clerk
e. experience
f. minimum wage
g. part-time
h. raise

When looking for a job, Melinda read the (1.) _____ in the newspaper. Because she didn't have any (2.) _____, Melinda knew that she had to start at the (3.) _____. Later she could get a (4.) _____. She called one store for an (5.) _____. The manager asked her to come in and fill out an (6.) _____. She was excited when she got the (7.) _____ job as a (8.) _____ in a clothing store.

# 10  A Part-Time Job

It's Friday evening, Dave's first evening on the job at Tackett's Shoe Shop. Mr. Tackett is showing Dave the inventory of shoes. The shelves contain shoes of every size, color, and style.

"Wow!" exclaims Dave. "I didn't know there were so many kinds of shoes!"

"There are a lot, aren't there?" responds Mr. Tackett. "We keep a large stock of shoes in a variety of styles because people have very different tastes. For example, some women like sporty flats, such as these." Mr. Tackett picks up a penny loafer and hands it to Dave. "Other women prefer a dressy pump, such as this." He picks up a fancy high-heeled shoe to show Dave. "We try to keep a variety of shoes in stock."

"That makes sense," says Dave.

"Now, let's go out to the front and I'll show you how to wait on customers. Just watch me," says Mr. Tackett.

Dave follows Mr. Tackett out to the front and watches him approach a customer.

"May I help you, ma'am?"

"Yes," says the customer. "I'm looking for a dressy white shoe. Do you have anything like that?"

"Yes, we do, ma'am. Come this way, please." Mr. Tackett leads the customer to a chair. "Please have a seat. Let me check your shoe size, and I'll bring out several styles for you to try on."

"Oh, I already know my shoe size. It's size seven."

"Fine," says Mr. Tackett. "I'll be right back with some white pumps."

"Thank you."

Dave watches Mr. Tackett go to the back of the store and return with several pairs of white high-heeled shoes.

(*several hours later*)

"How did you like your first evening on the job?" asks Mr. Tackett as he and Dave close up the store.

"There sure is a lot to know!" responds Dave.

"Yes, there is," says Mr. Tackett. "But tomorrow is another day. See you at 10:00 A.M. tomorrow."

"Okay. Good night."

"Good night."

A. **Answer the following questions.**
1. What is Dave doing this evening?
2. What does Mr. Tackett show Dave first?
3. Why does Mr. Tackett keep a large variety of shoes in stock? What shoes does he show Dave?
4. What does Mr. Tackett show Dave next?
5. What kind of shoes does the customer want to see?
6. What information does Mr. Tackett need before he gets the shoes?
7. What does Mr. Tackett bring from the back of the store?
8. What do Mr. Tackett and Dave do several hours later?
9. What does Dave say about his new job?

**B. Complete the sentences with these vocabulary words. If necessary, change the form of a word to make it agree with the other parts of the sentence.**

a. dressy
b. flat
c. (to) have a seat
d. high-heeled
e. inventory
f. penny loafer
g. pump
h. sporty
i. style
j. taste

Marge was shopping for shoes with her friend Chris.
"What (1.) _____ are you looking for?" Chris asked.
"I need something (2.) _____ to wear with my new suit," Marge said. "I also want some comfortable (3.) _____ to wear with jeans."
"What about these (4.) _____?" asked Chris. "They're (5.) _____ and flat."
"Those are nice," answered Marge. "And here are some pretty red (6.) _____ (7.) _____ that will match my suit perfectly. This store has a great (8.) _____ of shoes."
"And you have great (9.) _____," said Chris. "(10.) _____, and I'll find a clerk to help you."

# 11 Getting to Know Tom and Jill

Melissa and Dave are going into the snack bar after school.

"Hey, Dave! Do you see that cute guy over there?"

"Who?" Dave looks around the room casually. Finally he sees the person that Melissa is talking about. "The guy in the red sweater? He's not that cute, Melissa."

"Oh, I think he is! Do you know his name?"

"No, I don't. But I do know that he usually comes to school with a gorgeous girl."

"Oh," replies Melissa glumly.

"Here she comes now!" says Dave, his eyes opening wide.

"She's not that gorgeous, Dave! Hey, I know her! She's in my Spanish class. Her name is Jill."

"That means you can introduce me to her, Melissa."

"We don't know each other very well, but I guess it's okay."

Dave and Melissa walk over to the table where Jill and her friend are sitting.

"Hi, Jill," says Melissa.

"Hi! How's it going?" asks Jill.

"Great!" says Melissa. "This is my brother Dave. We're new here in Briartown. We moved here about a month ago, and we're trying to meet people."

"That's great!" says Jill. "Why don't you sit down? This is my brother Tom."

Dave and Tom shake hands.

"Hi," says Dave.

"Hi," Tom responds. "How're you doing?"

"Good."

Next Melissa extends her hand to Tom. "Pleased to meet you," she says.

"Same here," replies Tom.

Dave and Melissa sit down at the table.

Tom says, "Jill and I like to stop here for a snack on our way home from school. The hamburgers and fries are really good."

"I think I'll have a hamburger," says Dave. "What about you, Melissa?"

"A strawberry frozen yogurt sounds good to me."

"Okay. Where's the waiter?"

### A. Answer the following questions.
1. Where are Melissa and Dave?
2. Melissa sees a cute guy. What does Dave say about him?
3. Is Dave interested in anyone at the snack bar? What does Melissa say about the girl?
4. What do Melissa and Dave do next?
5. What does Jill say to Melissa and Dave?
6. What do Dave and Melissa do?
7. What does Tom say about the snack bar?
8. What do Dave and Melissa want to eat?

B. **Complete the sentences with these vocabulary words. If necessary, change the form of a word to make it agree with the other parts of the sentence.**

a. casually
b. cute
c. fries
d. frozen yogurt
e. glumly

f. gorgeous
g. hamburger
h. (to) introduce
i. snack bar
j. waiter

1. Tim got a job as a _____ at the _____.
2. Sharon ordered a _____, _____, and a _____ for lunch.
3. Kyoko will _____ the _____ girl and the _____ guy to each other.
4. The students were dressed _____ in jeans and sweatshirts.
5. Hector sat _____ looking out the window at the rain.

# 12 A Day at the Beach

Melissa and Dave are getting ready to spend a day at the beach. Earlier they asked Jill and Tom to join them. They're just about ready to leave.

"Let's see," says Melissa. "I packed lunches for all four of us, a six-pack of soda, my swimsuit, towels, and a volleyball. Is that everything, Dave?"

"What about sunscreen?"

"Oh! I almost forgot! Dave, will you run upstairs and get it from the medicine cabinet?"

"Okay," responds Dave. "Why don't you start loading the car while I get the lotion?"

"Sure!" says Melissa. She picks up the picnic basket and cooler and moves toward the door.

A few minutes later, Dave and Melissa are on their way to pick up Tom and Jill. As he drives up to their apartment

building, Dave sees both of them waiting by the curb.

"Hi!" say Tom and Jill.

"Hi!" respond Dave and Melissa.

"Great day, huh?" asks Tom.

"It sure is!" says Dave. "I can't believe it's almost October, and it's still warm enough to swim. Hop into the car and let's get going! We don't want to waste any more of this gorgeous day!"

Jill and Tom get into the car, and they head toward the beach.

### A. Answer the following questions.

1. What are Melissa and Dave getting ready to do? Who is going with them?
2. What did Melissa pack?
3. What does Dave remind Melissa to bring? What does Melissa ask Dave to do?
4. What does Melissa do while Dave is upstairs?
5. Are Tom and Jill ready to go?
6. What does Dave say to Tom and Jill?

### B. Complete the sentences with these vocabulary words. If necessary, change the form of a word to make it agree with the other parts of the sentence.

a. beach
b. cooler
c. (to) hop
d. (to) load
e. medicine cabinet
f. picnic basket
g. soda
h. spring break
i. sunscreen
j. swimsuit

It is a beautiful day during the (1.) _____ and the Kim family decides to go to the (2.) _____. Mr. Kim tells the children to put on their (3.) _____. He puts some cans of (4.) _____ in a (5.) _____ with ice. Mrs. Kim (6.) _____ a (7.) _____ with sandwiches and fruit.

"Do we have everything?" she asks her husband.

"I think so," he answers.

"Oh, no we don't! I need to get the (8.) _____ from the (9.) _____," exclaims Mrs. Kim.

"Good thinking," Mr. Kim says. "The kids and I will take these things and (10.) _____ in the car while you get it."

## 13 Friendly Competition

Dave, Melissa, Jill, and Tom arrive at the beach an hour later. They pass a sign that says "Lake Sharon." After driving a short distance farther, Dave finds a place to park the car. Dave and Tom grab their swimsuits and jump out of the car.

"I see a building with rest rooms over there. We can change our clothes in the men's room," Tom says to Dave. The two friends head toward the building.

"Hey, guys!" Melissa yells after them. "You forgot everything in the trunk. Help us carry the food and the beach towels!"

Dave calls back, "We can get that stuff later. Right now I want to check out the water!" Then he says to Tom, "Sisters are such a pain sometimes!"

"I'll say!" Tom agrees.

Meanwhile, the two girls decide to leave everything in the car. "Let's just put on our swimsuits too," suggests Melissa. "Why should Dave and Tom have all the fun? We can make them get everything out of the car later!"

Soon the four friends are on the beach in their swimsuits. Dave and Tom run into the water.

"Yow!" yells Dave. "It's co-o-o-ld!"

"Get tough, man!" says Tom. "It's not so bad."

Dave dives into the water again and comes up for air with a grin. "Yeah! It's okay. Race you to the end of the dock!"

Both boys swim toward the end of the dock as fast as they can. Tom beats Dave by about five yards. He climbs up onto the dock and turns to laugh at Dave, who is just reaching the dock.

"Wow, Tom!" Dave exclaims as he climbs out of the water. "You're a good swimmer! Are you on the swim team at school?"

"As a matter of fact, I am," Tom says. "What about you? Are you interested in trying out for the team?"

"No, I don't think so. Swimming isn't my sport, but I'm on the basketball team."

"That's great!" exclaims Tom.

Just then the girls join their brothers at the end of the dock.

"Did you find a good place for us on the beach?" Dave asks Melissa.

"No, we wanted to check out the water first," she answers, smiling at Jill. "You guys can unload the car whenever you're ready."

## A. Answer the following questions.
1. When do the four friends arrive at the beach?
2. What do Dave and Tom do immediately?
3. What does Melissa yell to Dave and Tom?
4. What is Dave's response?
5. What do Melissa and Jill decide to do?
6. How does Dave react to the water? How does Tom react?
7. What do the two boys do next?
8. Who wins the race?
9. What do Dave and Tom talk about on the dock?
10. What does Dave ask Melissa?
11. What is Melissa's response?

## B. Complete the sentences with these vocabulary words. If necessary, change the form of a word to make it agree with the other parts of the sentence.

a. (to) change one's clothes
b. (to) check out
c. (to) climb
d. (to) come up for air
e. (to) dive
f. dock
g. (to) grab
h. (to) park
i. (to) race
j. rest room
k. trunk
l. (to) unload

Suzanne and Sarah drove to the beach one afternoon. After Suzanne (1.) _____ the car, the two girls (2.) _____ their swimsuits and (3.) _____ to the (4.) _____.

"After we (5.) _____, let's go out on the (6.) _____," suggested Sarah.

"Okay," agreed Suzanne. "We can (7.) _____ the (8.) _____ later."

In a few minutes, Suzanne and Sarah were standing on the dock.

"The water looks cold," said Suzanne.

"Well, why don't you (9.) _____ it _____?" asked Sarah, pushing her friend gently into the lake. "Is it cold?" she asked with a smile when Suzanne (10.) _____.

"Come on in and find out!" invited Suzanne, laughing.

Sarah (11.) _____ gracefully into the water to join her friend. The two girls swam and splashed in the water for an hour before (12.) _____ out to rest on the beach.

# 14 Three's a Crowd

It is midafternoon. The four friends finished their picnic lunch an hour ago after spending the morning swimming and playing volleyball. Now they are sunning on the beach and sipping cans of soda. Melissa is lying on her beach towel with her eyes closed. Jill, Tom, and Dave are talking.

"Hey, what do you think about our new basketball coach, Dave?" asks Tom.

"So far, so good," responds Dave. "Since we're so new in town, I never met the old coach, you know. What do you think?"

"He's okay," replies Tom. "I did hear some of the guys talking about how tough he is."

"That's true," says Dave. "He doesn't put up with any goofing off. It's all business!"

At this point, Jill complains, "All you guys ever talk about is sports! There are other things in the world, you know!"

"Sorry!" shrugs Dave with a grin. "Do you want to go for a walk, Jill?"

"Sure. That sounds great! Just show me the way!"

Dave and Jill get up and start toward the road that surrounds the lake. Tom lies back on his beach towel for a few minutes. He looks over at Melissa, who seems to be asleep. Then he gets up and follows Dave and Jill.

"Hey, wait up, guys! You don't mind if I come along, do you?"

**A. Answer the following questions.**
1. What did the four friends do in the morning? What are they doing now?
2. What are Dave, Tom, and Jill talking about?
3. What does Tom say about the new coach?
4. Is Jill interested in sports? What does she say?
5. What does Dave suggest?
6. What does Tom do? What does he say?

**B. Complete the sentences with these vocabulary words. If necessary, change the form of a word to make it agree with the other parts of the sentence.**

a. all business    e. to sip
b. coach          f. to sun
c. (to) goof off   g. to surround
d. to shrug

1. Marco spent the afternoon _____ in the yard and _____ iced tea.
2. When Denise yelled at Tony for _____, Tony _____ his shoulders and said, "Hey! Volleyball is fun. It is not _____."
3. The basketball _____ told his team to _____ the player with the ball.

# 15 Dating: Part 1

Melissa and Dave drop Jill and Tom off at their home. They cheerfully wave good-bye as their car moves down the street and turns the corner. Then Melissa turns to Dave and asks, "What happened back at the lake this afternoon?"

"Nothing," responds Dave. He continues driving.

"Well, you seemed furious when you came back from your walk with Tom and Jill. You were glaring and you hardly said a word. What happened?"

"Well, nothing really," repeats Dave. "It's just that all day I was planning to spend some time alone with Jill. I really like her a lot, and we hardly had a chance to talk."

"Oh, I see!" nods Melissa.

"Her brother did all the talking for her," Dave continues. "And he never even let her out of his sight! I had no idea that he was so protective of her!"

"I didn't either," responds Melissa. Then she adds, "Well, how do you think *I* felt when Tom left me alone to join you and Jill?"

"You're right, Melissa," says Dave.

"I was hoping to talk with him a little, but the only thing he seemed interested in was sports. One reason why he followed you and Jill was to continue your conversation about basketball."

"Yeah. You're right." After pausing a moment, Dave tells Melissa, "Well anyway, I am going to ask Jill to the school dance next month. I'm not going to give up easily."

"Good for you, Dave!" exclaims Melissa. "Now let me know if you have any ideas about how I can get a date with Tom."

"I will," promises Dave, "but it's probably hopeless. You're so weird!" He laughs as Melissa pretends to punch him in the arm. "I'm just kidding. You're a terrific person, Melissa, and I know that a lot of guys would like to date you."

"Do you think so? Well, even so, I want to go out with Tom!"

"I know," says Dave, "but you will have to be patient! Right now, it's getting late. Let's get home. We can talk more about the dance later."

"It's a deal!" agrees Melissa.

### A. Answer the following questions.

1. After they drop off Tom and Jill, what do Dave and Melissa do?
2. Why was Dave furious after his walk with Tom and Jill? How did he act?
3. Who did all the talking for Jill while they were on their walk?
4. Why didn't Tom let Jill out of his sight?
5. Why is Melissa disappointed?
6. What does Tom seem interested in?
7. What does Dave plan to do?
8. Whom does Melissa want to date? What does she ask her brother?
9. What does Dave say in response?

**B. Complete the sentences with these vocabulary words. If necessary, change the form of a word to make it agree with the other parts of the sentence.**

a. cheerfully
b. date
c. (to) drop off
d. furious
e. (to) glare
f. (to) go out
g. kidding
h. patient
i. protective
j. sight
k. (to) wave
l. weird

Last week Bill made a (1.) _____ with Lisa after months of wanting to (2.) _____ with her. He was very excited when she agreed to go to the school dance with him. "You're (3.) _____!" he exclaimed after she said yes. "That's great!"

After the dance Bill was (4.) _____, because he barely got a chance to talk to Lisa all evening. Her brother was also at the dance, and he was so (5.) _____ that he hardly let Lisa out of his (6.) _____.

When Bill (7.) _____ Lisa at her home, she (8.) _____ good-bye to him (9.) _____. As he drove home, he (10.) _____ at the street in anger. Then he told himself, "Be (11.) _____, Bill. Her brother may be (12.) _____, but he'll accept me in time."

# 16 Dating: Part 2

It is one week later. Melissa is sitting in the snack bar waiting for Dave after school. In a few minutes he arrives and sits down next to her.

"Hi!" he says.

"Hi! How's it going?"

"Okay." He pauses. "I saw Jill in the library today."

"And?"

"Well, we studied together for about an hour."

"That's great, Dave!" exclaims Melissa.

"It's not so great, Melissa! I never got up enough nerve to ask her to the dance!"

"Oh!" responds Melissa. Then she adds, "Well, that's okay. You're getting to know her better, aren't you?"

"Yes, I am," admits Dave.

"Well, just call her up this evening. The worst that can happen is that she'll say no."

"Easier said than done, Melissa," says Dave glumly.

"I know, but at least you can ask her! I'm having to drop little hints to Tom about the dance."

"Oh, Melissa, why don't you just ask him to go with you? It's okay for a girl to ask a boy for a date!"

"Do you really think so?"

"Yes, I do," says Dave.

"Well, wait till you hear this! This morning I saw Tom between classes. I asked him if he was planning to go to watch your basketball game this afternoon."

"That's good," says Dave.

"Do you know what he said?"

"No."

"Well, he said that he was planning to go and that his girlfriend Marsha would stop by, too! See, Dave! At least you have a chance with Jill!"

"I'm sorry, Melissa! I didn't know Tom had a girlfriend. He never mentioned her."

"I know," reflects Melissa. "I guess I'll have to go with some girlfriends to the dance. You never know. I might meet someone nice there."

"Sure you will!" replies Dave. "And thanks for the encouragement about Jill."

"Don't mention it," says Melissa sadly.

### A. Answer the following questions.
1. Where do Dave and Melissa meet?
2. What did Dave do today? Why is he disappointed?
3. What does Melissa suggest?
4. Why is Melissa unhappy? What did she learn about that morning?
5. Does Dave think it's okay for a girl to ask a boy for a date?
6. What does Melissa decide to do about the dance?

**B. Complete the sentences with these vocabulary words. If necessary, change the form of a word to make it agree with the other parts of the sentence.**

a. (to) call up
b. (to) drop a hint
c. easier said
d. encouragement
e. glumly
f. library
g. (to) mention
h. nerve

Yesterday, Robert studied near Valerie in the (1.) _____. He (2.) _____ the school dance to her, but he never got up enough (3.) _____ to ask her to go with him. Now he is thinking about (4.) _____ Valerie _____ on the phone. But actually telephoning her is (5.) _____ than done. His older sister, Sarah, sees him sitting (6.) _____ by the phone. She says, "Robert, what's wrong?"

"Well," replies Robert, "I'm trying to call Valerie so I can (7.) _____ about the school dance."

"Oh," responds Sarah, "don't try to drop hints. Just ask her. You're a lot of fun. I'm sure she'll be happy to go to the dance with you."

"You're right. Thanks for the (8.) _____. I needed it. Now I think I'll call and ask Valerie to the dance!"

# 17 Expect the Unexpected

Dave is elated. After waiting a week, he finally asked Jill to the dance, and she accepted. As she resolved to do earlier, Melissa is planning to go to the dance with her girlfriends.

On the Tuesday before the dance, Melissa is stopping at her locker to pick up her books for the next class. As she heads toward her classroom, Tom walks up to her.

"Hi, Melissa," he grins. "I'm going this way, too."

"Oh, hi," stammers Melissa, surprised to see Tom. They walk slowly down the hall without talking. At the door to Melissa's classroom, Tom says, "Hey, Melissa! I wanted to ask you something. Will you go to the dance with me on Saturday? . . . I know that Dave is going with Jill. Maybe we could double-date."

"But what about . . . ?" starts Melissa.

Tom interrupts her. "You're wondering about Marsha, aren't you?"

Melissa nods.

Tom goes on: "Marsha and I had a long talk last Saturday. We decided to stop dating. Both of us agreed that it was better that way."

Melissa listens quietly.

"So," Tom continues, "will you go to the dance with me?"

Melissa smiles. "Tom, I'll be happy to go to the dance with you. And I'm sure that Dave will be interested in double-dating. Do you want to talk to him about it, or shall I?"

"Why don't you talk to him first? After all, he's your brother," responds Tom. "Then I'll call him this evening to follow up. How does that sound?"

"It sounds great," replies Melissa.

"Good! Okay, then. It's a date, right?" asks Tom, flashing her a grin.

"Right," responds Melissa. "See you later."

"Bye."

"Bye."

**A. Answer the following questions.**
1. Did Jill accept Dave's invitation to the dance? How does he feel?
2. Earlier, what did Melissa resolve to do?
3. What is Melissa doing at her locker on Tuesday?
4. Who walks up to her? What does he say? What do they do?
5. What does Tom ask Melissa?
6. What does Melissa wonder about? What is Tom's explanation?
7. Does Melissa accept the invitation?
8. Who is going to speak to Dave first about double-dating? Who will follow up?

**B. Complete the sentences with these vocabulary words. If necessary, change the form of a word to make it agree with the other parts of the sentence.**

a. (to) double-date    e. locker
b. elated    f. (to) resolve
c. (to) follow up    g. (to) stammer
d. grin

On Monday Matt (1.) _____ to talk with Keiko. He saw her at her (2.) _____ and walked over to her. He (3.) _____ nervously, "How's it going, Keiko?" Then he flashed her a (4.) _____.

Keiko smiled. "Hi, Matt. I'm fine."

"Are you going to class now?" he asked.

"Yes, let's go!" she said.

As they walked down the hall together, Matt felt (5.) _____. "Now I can (6.) _____ by asking her to the football game," he thought. "Maybe we can (7.) _____ with Tim and his girlfriend."

# 18 The School Dance

The evening of the dance arrives at last. Jill and Tom stop at the Jacksons' house to pick up Dave and Melissa. They are sitting in the living room with Mr. and Mrs. Jackson when Dave and Melissa join them.

After the greetings, Dave sits down next to Jill on the sofa and says, "I have a surprise for you, Jill."

"Really? What is it?" she asks.

Dave hands her a beautiful corsage.

"It's lovely, Dave!" exclaims Jill with pleasure. "I'll pin it on my dress. Oh, I have something for you, too." Jill hands Dave a small flower to pin on his jacket.

"Thanks, Jill. This is great," says Dave uncertainly. "Do all the guys wear these?"

"Sure they do," laughs Melissa as she gives Tom a similar flower.

"Thanks," says Tom. "I hope you like this wrist corsage."

"What pretty colors!" Melissa smiles as she slips the elastic band over her right wrist.

"Well," says Mrs. Jackson, "I guess it's time for the four of you to be on your way." Mr. Jackson nods in agreement.

The parents walk the couples to the car. Tom opens the front door for Melissa and Dave opens the back door for Jill, and they all say good-bye.

After watching the four young people drive off, Mr. Jackson turns to his wife and says, "Helen, our kids sure are growing up, aren't they?"

"Yes, they are," replies Mrs. Jackson. "I hope they have a wonderful evening."

**A. Answer the following questions.**
1. What evening is it?
2. Who is at the Jacksons' house? Why?
3. Where are they sitting? Who is with them?
4. What does Dave give Jill?
5. What does Jill give Dave? How does he feel about it?
6. What does Tom give Melissa? Where does she wear it?
7. Who walks the two couples to the car?
8. Who rides in the front seat? Who rides in the back seat?
9. What does Mr. Jackson say to his wife, Helen, as the couples drive away?
10. What is Mrs. Jackson's reaction?

**B. Complete the sentences with these vocabulary words. If necessary, change the form of a word to make it agree with the other parts of the sentence.**

a. corsage
b. elastic band
c. (to) hand
d. living room
e. pleasure
f. sofa
g. surprise
h. uncertainly
i. wrist

James and Lisa often double-date with Tim and Susan. Tonight they are going to the senior dance. James comes to pick up Lisa. When Lisa enters the (1.) _____, James is sitting on the (2.) _____ with a wide grin on his face. He has a (3.) _____ for her—a beautiful (4.) _____. James (5.) _____ Lisa the corsage.

"It's so beautiful," she exclaims with (6.) _____. "Will you pin it on my dress?" Then she notices an (7.) _____ under the flower. "Is this a (8.) _____ corsage, James?"

James shrugs his shoulders (9.) _____. "Gosh, Lisa, I'm not sure!"

# 19 Some Exciting News

It is the Monday following the dance, Melissa is again at her locker when Tom comes up to speak to her.

"I had a great time at the dance, Melissa," says Tom as they move down the hall toward Melissa's classroom.

"So did I! . . . Wasn't the band great?"

"It sure was!" exclaims Tom. "I didn't realize that the Jets could play anything besides rock music. But, wow! They played great forties and fifties music, too!"

"It was fun, wasn't it?" answers Melissa.

"It was fun to dance with you, too, Melissa," says Tom. "Thanks."

As they approach her classroom, Melissa turns to Tom to share some exciting news. "Tom, we invited an international student to live with us next semester. Her name is Carmen; she is from Peru."

"Hey, that's neat! When does she get here?"

"She'll be here in another month," replies Melissa. "We plan to have a welcoming party for her, and we hope you and Jill will come."

"Of course we will! Just tell us the date and time, and we'll be there!"

"Great!" replies Melissa.

"Let us know how we can help, too!" adds Tom. "We don't want to leave you and Dave with all the work!"

"Thanks. We'll definitely need some help with the party, so I appreciate your offer."

"It's time for class to begin. See you later!" says Tom.

"Bye, Tom. Thanks again for a nice evening on Saturday."

**A. Answer the following questions.**
1. Whom does Melissa see at her locker?
2. What do Tom and Melissa talk about as they walk to class together?
3. What was the name of the band that played at the dance? What kind of music did the band play?
4. What exciting news does Melissa share with Tom?
5. How will the Jackson family welcome Carmen when she arrives?
6. What does Tom offer to do?

**B. Complete the sentences with these vocabulary words. If necessary, change the form of a word to make it agree with the other parts of the sentence.**
   a. forties and fifties   d. rock
   b. international         e. semester
   c. party

It is the beginning of the (1.) _____, and Paula is hosting a (2.) _____ for the new (3.) _____ student, Ilya. Paula's friend Kumi brings over some tapes to play during the party. These include both (4.) _____ music and (5.) _____ music.

# 20 The Welcoming Party

The month is passing quickly. Melissa and Dave send out invitations to their teachers and friends, asking them to attend the party and to welcome Carmen to Briartown. In preparation for the party, Tom and Jill bring over some of their favorite tapes. Tom and Jill will go with the Jacksons to meet Carmen at the airport when she arrives.

Carmen arrives on the Thursday before the party. She and Melissa become friends immediately. Carmen is more shy around Dave but shows that she likes him, too.

On Saturday, Mrs. Jackson, Melissa, and Carmen prepare the refreshments. Dave and his father pick up the house and decorate the patio. Soon after 7:00 P.M., the doorbell rings.

"Dave, will you get the door, please?" calls Mrs. Jackson from the kitchen.

"Sure!" says Dave. He opens the door and greets Mr. Rodriguez, the school principal.

"Hello, Mr. Rodriguez. You are the first person to arrive. Come on in, please, and meet Carmen."

They walk into the living room, where Carmen is sitting with Mr. Jackson. Mr. Jackson gets up to greet Mr. Rodriguez. "Good evening! We're so glad you can be with us to welcome Carmen."

"Thank you for inviting me," responds Mr. Rodriguez. He turns toward Carmen, "And here is our newest student! Carmen, I'm Mr. Rodriguez, the principal of Lincoln High School. We are delighted that you will be studying with us this semester!"

"How do you do, sir," responds Carmen, standing up to shake his hand.

In a few minutes, the living room is filled with people. Each guest comes over to greet Carmen.

"Thank you," Carmen responds. "I'm very happy to be here!"

### A. Answer the following questions.

1. To whom do Dave and Melissa send invitations?
2. When does Carmen arrive? Who meets her at the airport?
3. Who prepares the refreshments for the party? Who picks up the house and decorates the patio?
4. Who arrives at the door first? Who greets him at the door?
5. What does Mr. Rodriguez say when he meets Carmen?
6. How does Carmen greet Mr. Rodriguez?
7. What happens within the next few minutes?

**B. Complete the sentences with these vocabulary words. If necessary, change the form of a word to make it agree with the other parts of the sentence.**

a. (to) decorate   f. (to) pick up
b. delighted      g. (to) prepare
c. (to) greet     h. refreshments
d. guest          i. tape
e. invitation     j. welcome

Paula sent out the (1.) _____ to her party two weeks ago. Most of her friends are planning to attend. Paula is (2.) _____ with the response from her (3.) _____.

Today Paula and her family (4.) _____ the house, (5.) _____ the patio, and (6.) _____ refreshments for the party this evening. Kumi's (7.) _____ will be playing as the guests arrive.

While Paula and her mother are putting the last (8.) _____ on the table, her father is (9.) _____ the guests. He makes them feel (10.) _____ by giving each one a friendly handshake.

# 21 Carmen and Jill Become Friends

The party is well under way when Jill and Tom arrive. Dave greets them at the door.

"Hi, guys! Come on in!"

"Sorry we're late," says Jill. "We had some car trouble."

"Yeah!" adds Tom. "We had a flat tire on the way here. I put on the spare tire, and then we drove to a gas station. The attendant patched our tire and put it back on."

"Wow!" exclaims Dave. "What a start for the evening! Well, come on in and greet everyone. Carmen seems to be having a good time."

Jill and Tom walk with Dave into the living room. Carmen immediately gets up and walks across the room to greet them.

"Jill and Tom," she smiles, "I'm so happy to see you again!"

"It's nice to see you, too," says Tom.

Taking Carmen by the arm, Jill asks, "Well, who did you meet before we arrived? I see lots of friends and teachers from school here."

"I think I met everyone. First, I met Mr. Rodriguez. He is very friendly, isn't he?"

"Yes, he is," answers Jill. "When you come to school on Monday, he will be very helpful. . . . Just ask Dave and Melissa. At the beginning of the school year, they were new here in Briartown. He made them feel very welcome. And now, look at them!" Jill waves her hand in their direction. "You couldn't be staying with a nicer family!"

"I know," says Carmen. "I'm lucky. They are wonderful to me. It really helps, because I miss my own family in Peru very much."

"I know you do. Well, let's go get some refreshments, okay?"

"Okay!"

The girls head toward the refreshment table. Al Flores, the junior class president, is standing near it.

### A. Answer the following questions.
1. Why do Tom and Jill arrive late?
2. What does Carmen do when she sees Tom and Jill?
3. What does Jill ask Carmen?
4. How does Carmen describe Mr. Rodriguez?
5. What does Jill say about Dave and Melissa?
6. Does Carmen consider herself lucky? How does she feel about living with the Jacksons?
7. Whom does Carmen miss?

**B. Complete the sentences with these vocabulary words. If necessary, change the form of a word to make it agree with the other parts of the sentence.**

a. attendant  e. (to) miss
b. flat tire  f. (to) patch
c. friendly  g. spare tire
d. helpful  h. under way

1. If your car has a _____, you need to put on the _____.
2. Claudia, the new international student, _____ her family.
3. The _____ students welcomed Jorge to their school.
4. Ms. Valdivia, the principal, is _____ to all the students at Kennedy High School.
5. The party was well _____ when they began serving refreshments.
6. The gas station _____ can _____ your tire.

## 22 Carmen Meets Mrs. Schroeder

"Hi, Al," says Jill. "Have you met Carmen Calderon? She is our new international student from Peru. Carmen, this is Al Flores, our class president."

"Pleased to meet you, Carmen," says Al.

"I am pleased to meet you, too," responds Carmen.

Because Al speaks Spanish, Carmen talks with him in her native language while Jill gets fruit punch for Carmen and herself. Jill returns with the drinks and asks, "Al, can I get you some punch?"

"Oh, no thanks, Jill. Carmen, it sure was good to meet you. Let me know if you have any questions when you get to school on Monday. Maybe we'll be in some of the same classes."

"Okay! I'll see you later," responds Carmen.

"Let's talk to some more people," suggests Jill. The two girls move toward a teacher who is talking with a group of students.

"Mrs. Schroeder, this is Carmen Calderon, our new international student."

"We met a few minutes ago, but we didn't really have time to talk," says Mrs. Schroeder. "Did you just arrive in the United States, Carmen?"

"Yes, on Thursday," Carmen answers. "I'm living with Mr. and Mrs. Jackson and Melissa and Dave. I will start school on Monday."

"That's wonderful, Carmen!" exclaims Mrs. Schroeder. "I hope that you will consider taking my speech or my drama class. Either one would be fun for you. You would get lots of practice in speaking English."

"I need practice. Thank you," says Carmen.

"As a matter of fact, here are several of my best students," continues Mrs. Schroeder. "This is James Washington."

"I am pleased to meet you, James," says Carmen.

"Hi, Carmen," says James.

"Linda Chau," continues Mrs. Schroeder.

"Hello, Linda," says Carmen.

"Hi," responds Linda. "I hope you'll join our class."

"Thank you. It sounds wonderful," responds Carmen.

"This is Skip Harrison. He is playing the lead in our new play, *Brighton Beach Memoirs*."

"Hello, Skip," says Carmen.

"Hi!" says Skip. "Hope to see you in class."

"It's very nice to meet all of you. Thank you very much, Mrs. Schroeder," says Carmen. "I will seriously consider taking one of your courses."

"Good!" answers Mrs. Schroeder.

"Well, let's give others a chance to talk to Carmen," says Jill. "Thanks, Mrs. Schroeder. Enjoy the party, everybody!"

A. **Answer the following questions.**
1. Whom does Carmen meet at the refreshment table? In what language do they start speaking?
2. Which teacher does Carmen meet next? What subjects does she teach?
3. What does Mrs. Schroeder encourage Carmen to do? Why?
4. Mrs. Schroeder introduces Carmen to several of her students. What are their names?
5. What is Skip Harrison doing in *Brighton Beach Memoirs,* the new play?
6. What does Carmen tell Mrs. Schroeder?

B. **Complete the sentences with these vocabulary words. If necessary, change the form of a word to make it agree with the other parts of the sentence.**
a. (to) consider    d. lead
b. drama            e. native language
c. fruit punch      f. speech

1. The _____ teacher encouraged Scott to take her course. Soon he was _____ trying out for the _____ in the school play.
2. The _____ teacher's _____ is Japanese.
3. Did you taste the _____? It is wonderful!

# 23 Family Matters

Today Carmen completed her first day at Lincoln High School. Now she and the Jackson family are sitting around the dinner table.

"Well, how did it go today, Carmen?" asks Mr. Jackson.

"It was fine," responds Carmen. "Dave and Melissa helped me find my classes at school."

"Good!" exclaims Mr. Jackson. "What courses are you taking?"

"I'm taking English, Algebra II, and American History, and I'm also taking Choir, PE, and Drama."

"Boy! You are going to have a full schedule, Carmen!" says Mrs. Jackson.

"I know, but Mr. Rodriguez said that I should try this schedule for two weeks. If it's too much, I can change it."

"That's fair enough!" replies Mr. Jackson.

"I know that with these courses my English will improve, too," adds Carmen.

"Another good point!" responds Mr. Jackson, turning next to Dave. Melissa and Dave glance at each other.

"And how was your day, son?"

"Oh, fine, Dad. I worked some extra hours at Mr. Tackett's store this afternoon."

"I didn't know that," muses Mr. Jackson. "Don't you think you're working at the store a little too much these days?"

"Aw, Dad!" responds Dave. "You know that I'm trying to make enough money to buy a car, and . . ."

"I know, David," interrupts Mr. Jackson, "but a car is not more important than your studies. When you started this job, you agreed to work on Thursday and Friday evenings and on Saturdays. I think that's enough work for you right now."

"Oh, please!" protests Dave. "Mr. Tackett needs me on those extra days. What will I tell him when he asks me to work?"

"You'll tell him that your parents think you need to spend more time on your studies, and that you can work only on the days you originally agreed upon."

"I can't do that! He'll fire me!" exclaims Dave.

"Yes, you can, and no, he won't!" responds Mr. Jackson. "He will understand that your studies come before your job. . . . Take it or leave it. Either you cut back to the agreed-upon hours, or you'll have to quit your job!"

Dave sits silently looking down at his plate. After a few moments, he looks up and answers, "Okay, Dad. I don't think Mr. Tackett will like it, but I'll tell him the bad news on Thursday evening."

"Good, Dave!" responds Mr. Jackson. "Now, Melissa, how was your day?"

A. **Answer the following questions.**
1. What is the Jackson family doing?
2. How was Carmen's day? What did she do?
3. What subjects is Carmen taking? What is Mrs. Jackson's reaction to her schedule?

4. What did Mr. Rodriguez say about Carmen's schedule?
5. What does Mr. Jackson ask Dave? What is Dave's response?
6. Why is Mr. Jackson unhappy?
7. What two reasons does Dave give for continuing to work extra hours?
8. What is Mr. Jackson's final answer?
9. What does Dave agree to do?

B. **Complete the sentences with these vocabulary words. If necessary, change the form of a word to make it agree with the other parts of the sentence.**

a. algebra
b. choir
c. (to) complete
d. (to) cut back
e. (to) fire
f. (to) glance
g. (to) learn one's way around
h. (to) muse
i. news
j. (to) quit
k. take it or leave it

1. The children heard the bad _____ about their father losing his job. His boss became angry and _____ him.
2. Stanley is spending too much time playing football. He never _____ his homework assignments.
3. The manager offered James the job at $5.00 per hour, telling him, "_____." James decided to take the job, and soon he _____ the factory.
4. When Julia's boss _____ her hours, Julia _____ her job and found a new one.
5. When he was _____ over the _____ problem, Jack _____ up to see Joan looking at him. She walked over and said, "Excuse me for interrupting you, but do you understand this problem?"
6. The _____ practiced many hours before the concert.

# 24 The College Entrance Exam

Several months pass. All the juniors at Lincoln High School are getting ready to take their college exams. They began to prepare for the exams several months ago.

Melissa and Jill are in the library. The test will begin in a few minutes. Jill is still looking over her notes.

"Jill," whispers Melissa.

"Yes?" She looks up.

"Are you ready for the test?"

"I guess I'm as ready as I'm going to be," replies Jill.

"I'm so nervous," says Melissa.

"Don't worry. You should do well. I know you studied very hard. You'll do just fine!"

"I hope so," sighs Melissa.

Jill continues, "We both followed a study schedule, and that was the most important thing. Besides, last month we took the entrance exam preparation course. And you continued to study those test manuals, didn't you?"

Melissa nods.

"See, you'll be fine," Jill reassures her. "What you need to do now is relax!"

"You're right, Jill." Melissa gets up and walks around the library. For a few minutes, she looks out the window at two birds in a tree nearby.

With her thoughts again on the task ahead, Melissa walks back to the table where she and Jill were studying.

"Are you ready to go?" she asks her friend.

"Sure!" says Jill. "Let's go!"

**A. Answer the following questions.**
1. Who is studying to take the college entrance exam?
2. Where are Jill and Melissa now? What are they doing?
3. How does Jill feel about the exam? How does Melissa feel about it?
4. What is Jill's advice to Melissa?
5. What does Melissa do next? What does she see?

**B. Complete the sentences with these vocabulary words. If necessary, change the form of a word to make it agree with the other parts of the sentence.**

a. college entrance exam
b. entrance exam preparation course
c. library
d. manual
e. nervous
f. (to) reassure
g. (to) relax
h. task
i. (to) worry

All the juniors at Kennedy High School were studying for their (1.) _____. Many of them took the (2.) _____ last month. Today they were reviewing their test (3.) _____ in the (4.) _____. Because several of them seemed (5.) _____, the English teacher, Mr. Smith, was (6.) _____ them. He said, "Don't (7.) _____ about the exams. If you studied the test manuals thoroughly, you can (8.) _____. Soon your (9.) _____ will be finished."

# 25 Planning for College

The Jackson family is again sitting at the dinner table. Melissa and Carmen are chatting about the new school play. Dave and his father are talking about last evening's basketball game. Soon Melissa notices that her mother is very quiet.

"Are you feeling okay, Mom?" she asks.

"Yes, I'm okay," Mrs. Jackson says. "I was just thinking about something I want to discuss with all of you."

The table grows quiet. Everyone looks at Mrs. Jackson.

"Is something wrong, Mom?" asks Dave. He looks worried.

"No, no," Mrs. Jackson reassures him. "I just have some news to tell you. Actually, I hope you'll be happy about it." She pauses and glances around the table. "I think the time is

63

right for me to get a job. I enjoy being at home and taking care of all of you, but you're growing up very quickly. You're busy with school and your other activities. Next year Dave will be starting college, and the year after that Melissa will go away to school, too. I enjoyed my accounting work before you kids were born, and I think I'm ready to go back to it."

"That's great, Mom!" says Dave.

"Will you work part-time or full-time?" asks Melissa.

"I'm not sure yet. I'll have to see what's available."

"Your mother also wants to earn money to help pay for your college expenses, kids," says Mr. Jackson. "The next few years will be very expensive for us, especially when both of you are in college at the same time."

"That's true," says Melissa. "Dave and I can help save money, too."

"Yeah," says Dave. "I guess I can save what I earn at Mr. Tackett's store for college instead of for a car." He looks a bit unhappy.

"That's a nice idea, Dave, but we know how much you want your own car," says Mr. Jackson. "Why don't you save half your money for college and half for a car? That way you can still get a car—you'll just have to wait a little longer."

Dave looks relieved. "No problem, Dad."

"Can I get a job, too?" asks Melissa.

"Why don't you wait until school's out and then get a summer job?" Mrs. Jackson suggests.

"That's a good idea. Maybe I can get a job at the mall."

"When are you going to start working, Mom?" asks Dave.

"I'll start putting my résumé together as soon as I can. Then I'll just have to find the right job."

"Maybe I should get a job, too," Carmen suggests. Everyone laughs.

"You'll have to talk to your parents about that when you go back to Peru," says Mrs. Jackson.

### A. Answer the following questions.

1. What is the Jackson family doing?
2. What does Melissa notice?
3. What is Mrs. Jackson's news?
4. Why does Mrs. Jackson want to get a job?

5. Why will the next few years be expensive for the Jacksons?
6. What does Dave offer to do?
7. What does Mr. Jackson suggest to Dave?
8. What does Melissa decide to do?
9. What does Carmen suggest?

**B. Complete the sentences with these vocabulary words. If necessary, change the form of a word to make it agree with the other parts of the sentence.**

a. accounting   f. (to) glance
b. available    g. mall
c. (to) chat    h. relieved
d. expense      i. résumé
e. expensive    j. (to) save

Marty went shopping at the (1.) _____ on Saturday. He was looking for a new jacket, but all the jackets he saw were too (2.) _____. He decided to try one last store before going home. As he walked up to the store, he (3.) _____ in the window and saw a big sign. It said, "(4.) _____ money now on spring jackets!" Inside the store, Marty was (5.) _____ to find many styles (6.) _____ in his size. He chose the one he liked best and took it to the checkout counter.

Marty paid for the jacket and walked back into the mall. He saw his cousin Emily talking with a group of her friends. Marty went over to see her, and the cousins (7.) _____ for a few minutes.

"What's new with you, Emily?" Marty asked.

"Well, I'll be graduating from college soon, so I'm putting together my (8.) _____. I want to get a job with an (9.) _____ company."

"Good luck!" said Marty. "I got a part-time job a few months ago, to help Mom and Dad pay for my college (10.) _____. I can hardly wait to start at the university this fall!"

# 26 The Family Trip

The school year is over, and it is almost time for Carmen to return to Peru. The Jacksons are going to take a family vacation before Carmen leaves them. After their trip, Mrs. Jackson and Melissa will start their new jobs.

On the morning of the departure, the family is ready to go by seven o'clock. They all packed their luggage the day before in order to get an early start, and Mr. Jackson supervised the packing of the car. Now he is at the wheel ready to go. Mrs. Jackson is sitting beside him in the front seat.

"Come on! Get in the car!" yells Dave to Melissa and Carmen. They get in the back seat with him.

"Okay, is everybody ready?" asks Mr. Jackson.

They all nod in agreement.

"Then we're off!" Mr. Jackson pulls out of the driveway and heads toward the freeway.

The family will spend ten days touring the New England states. They plan to drive north first, through the Finger Lakes region of New York. Then they will head east toward Massachusetts, where they will visit Boston, Plymouth, and Salem. Next they will go north through New Hampshire and into Maine. They will be back in Briartown a week from Saturday.

"I am so excited about this trip!" exclaims Carmen.

"So are we," responds Melissa. "This is the first time we will be seeing this area, although it is quite near. And I'm so glad that we'll be sharing this trip with you, Carmen!"

"We are all glad, Carmen," adds Mrs. Jackson. "You know that we're going to miss you very much."

"I know, and I'll miss you, too," Carmen answers.

"You must come back for a visit someday," says Mrs. Jackson.

"I will," promises Carmen.

"And maybe someday we could visit you!" suggests Dave.

"That would be wonderful!" Carmen tells him.

A. **Answer the following questions.**
   1. What time of year is it?
   2. What did the Jackson family decide to do? Why?
   3. At what time of day do they leave on their trip?
   4. Where do Dave, Melissa, and Carmen sit? Who is in the front seat?
   5. To what state will the family drive first? After that, which state will they visit?
   6. Finally, through what two states will they drive?
   7. For what two reasons is Melissa excited about the trip?
   8. Will Carmen miss the Jackson family when she returns home to Peru? Will they miss her?
   9. What does Carmen promise to do?

**B. Use the map below to help you complete the sentences with these vocabulary words. If necessary, change the form of a word to make it agree with the other parts of the sentence.**

a. Boston
b. luggage
c. Maine
d. New Hampshire
e. Plymouth
f. (to) promise
g. Salem

Mr. and Mrs. Robbins (1.) _____ their family a vacation to New England. One morning in early June, they packed their (2.) _____ in the car and headed toward New York State. After passing the Finger Lakes, they turned east and drove toward Massachusetts. In that state, they visited the cities of (3.) _____, (4.) _____, and (5.) _____, where there were many interesting historical sites. Next, they drove north through the states of (6.) _____ and (7.) _____. They had a wonderful vacation.

# 27 A Special Dinner

After a wonderful vacation, the Jackson family is on its way home. In Massachusetts, they visited historical sites in Boston, Salem, and Plymouth. In New Hampshire, they traveled through the beautiful White Mountains. This evening, they are traveling down the coast and they stop to eat in a restaurant overlooking the Atlantic Ocean.

"What can I get everyone to drink?" asks the waiter.

Mr. and Mrs. Jackson order coffee, and the three young people order lemonade.

When the waiter returns with the beverages, Mr. Jackson

asks, "What do you recommend from the menu? We're just traveling through, and we want to try the specialty of the house."

"Certainly!" responds the waiter. "The fresh Maine lobster is our specialty, of course. We serve that with rice and vegetables. Our other seafood is excellent too. Another regional dish—if you like that sort of thing—is Boston baked beans with brown bread."

"There are a number of excellent choices, aren't there?" muses Mrs. Jackson.

"Yes, there are," responds the waiter. "May I suggest the lobster? It is the house specialty, and if you like lobster, you can't go wrong with it."

"Well Carmen, what sounds good to you?" asks Mr. Jackson. "This is a special dinner in your honor."

"Yes, it is!" they all agree.

"I love seafood," says Carmen, "so I think I'll try the lobster, because it will be a long time before I have a chance to taste it again."

Mr. and Mrs. Jackson also order the lobster, and Dave orders baked halibut. Melissa decides to try the Boston baked beans. Then after the waiter leaves, Melissa holds up her lemonade glass to make a toast.

"To Carmen! May she have a safe journey home, and may she come back to see us in the future!"

"To Carmen!" everyone responds.

"Thank you, everyone. I'll miss you very much. I promise to write you from Peru," says Carmen.

### A. Answer the following questions.
1. What are Carmen and the Jackson family doing? Where do they stop?
2. What did they see earlier on their trip?
3. What beverages do they order?
4. Why does Mr. Jackson ask the waiter to recommend a dish?
5. What dishes does the waiter suggest?
6. What do Carmen, Melissa, and Dave order?
7. What do Mr. and Mrs. Jackson order?
8. To whom does Melissa make a toast? What does she use?
9. What wish does she express for Carmen?

B. **Complete the sentences with these vocabulary words. If necessary, change the form of a word to make it agree with the other parts of the sentence.**

a. baked beans
b. beverage
c. coast
d. historical
e. lemonade
f. (to) make a toast
g. menu
h. (to) overlook
i. seafood
j. specialty

After visiting many interesting (1.) _____ sites on their vacation, the Robbins family headed home. On their drive along the (2.) _____, they stopped at a restaurant (3.) _____ the Atlantic Ocean. There they all asked for glasses of (4.) _____ to drink. After the waiter served them their (5.) _____, he passed out the (6.) _____. He also recommended several (7.) _____ of the house. He recommended Maine lobster as the most popular (8.) _____ dish. In addition, he suggested Boston (9.) _____ with brown bread. The family ordered their food. Then they (10.) _____ to wonderful family vacations.